C000170666

DURHAM CITY

Philip Nixon

First published in Great Britain in 2011

British Library Cataloguing-in-Publication Data
A CIP record for this title is available from the British Library

ISBN 978 0 85710 030 6

PiXZ Books
Halsgrove House, Ryelands Business Park,
Bagley Road, Wellington, Somerset TA21 9PZ
Tel: 01823 653777
Fax: 01823 216796
email: sales@halsgrove.com

An imprint of Halstar Ltd, part of the Halsgrove group of companies
Information on all Halsgrove titles is available at: www.halsgrove.com

Printed and bound in China by Toppan Leefung Printing Ltd

Contents

	Introduction	4
1	**Finchale Priory Walk**	7
2	**Durham River Banks Walk**	11
3	**Houghall Circular Walk**	17
4	**Shincliffe Woods Walk**	23
5	**Observatory Hill Walk**	29
6	**Shincliffe Bridge Circular Walk**	35
7	**Kepier Wood Walk**	41
8	**Frankland Walk**	47
9	**Bearpark Walk**	53
10	**Pittington and Renny's Lane Walk**	59

Introduction

Durham is a good place to live. Because of its small size it offers all the advantages of a city without the disadvantages. These ten country walks are all within the boundary of the city and each stands as a walk by itself but with a bit of careful planning parts of two or even more can easily be combined to give a longer walk. For the most part these footpaths are easy going although as with all walking it is probably safer to wear boots or stout footwear – most are dog friendly and have been thoroughly tested and approved by Archie our family labrador.

Durham Cathedral and Castle and their surrounding buildings were designated one of Britain's first World Heritage Sites in November 1986 and they attract thousands of tourists a year. St Cuthbert's body was brought to Durham in 995 and a religious community flourished from then until the Reformation – Durham was closed as a priory on 31st December 1539 – even though St Cuthbert's shrine was still the most visited in Britain – and so for over 500 years these ancient tracks and pathways were probably used by the monks of Durham to visit such places as Beaurepaire, Hallgarth Church and Finchale Priory. After the closure at the Reformation the Cathedral was immediately reinstated as an Anglican Church and pilgrims continued to visit the shrine of St Cuthbert and during the late Middle Ages these tracks would be used by the numerous pilgrims on their sacred journeys. Many of them probably also served as drovers' roads along which cattle, sheep , goats, gissy-pigs and geese would all be driven to market.

Beyond the agricultural revolution and in to the industrial revolution with its advantages and consequences saw the coming of railways into the city – and many of these now disused railways make excellent and comfortable paths for walking.

It has been a great pleasure to produce this little book – for many years I have led photographic walks throughout the County as parts of Durham County Council's Walks Programme and it is nice to see some of them "in print", as it were, but hopefully this book will inspire both photographers and walkers to enjoy further exploration of the many varied footpaths around Durham City.

If you see a grumpy looking old chap with a labrador when on these walks it's probably me; so do stop and tell me how much you've enjoyed the book – if you haven't enjoyed it just hide behind a tree until I've passed…

Big thanks to:
Valerie Nixon, Mark Nixon, Sophy Nixon, Adrian Briggs, Archie the labrador, Brian Armstrong, Durham Johnston School, DCC Countryside selection and, of course, Simon Butler and Sharon O'Inn at Halsgrove.

Maps
Recommended maps are OS Landranger 88 and OS Pathfinder 572.

Key to Symbols Used

Level of difficulty:

Easy

Fair 🧡 🧡

More challenging 🧡 🧡 🧡

Map symbols:

🚗	Park & start
——	Road
- - -	Walk Footpath
■	Building / Town
+	Church
▲	Landmark
🚻	WC
🍴	Refreshments
🍺	Pub

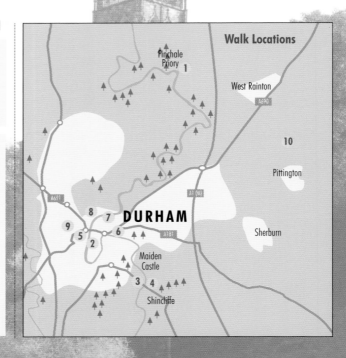

Walk Locations

Finchale Priory 1

West Rainton

A690

10

Pittington

A691

A1 (N)

8

9 5 7 **DURHAM**

6

A181

Sherburn

2

Maiden Castle

3 4

Shincliffe

1 **Finchale Priory Walk**

GR 297472

A short walk around the evocative Finchale Priory

Level:
Length: 1 mile.
Duration: Approx 1½ hours
Park and Start: At Finchale Abbey campsite. £2.50 charge. NZ294470
Refreshments: The shop/café situated beside the priory

This short but pleasant walk of about a mile, takes about an hour and a half including an exploration of the ruins of Finchale (pronounced 'Finkle) Priory. The buildings and immediate grounds are in the care of English Heritage – the further environs have been developed as Finchale Abbey Caravan Park – an award-winning eco village project set up to sustainably manage development in the area. Entry to the site is through an automated barrier. The caravan site has many modern luxuries and the southern approaches are a working farm. However, this is still an isolated site, situated at the far extremity of a dead-end road contained by thick woodland and the steep cliffs on the far banks of the River Wear.

It was St Godric who established a hermitage dedicated to St John the Baptist on the original site in the early twelfth century. Godric's biographer recorded that he lived a difficult and frugal life on this "snake

Cocken Road

Cocken Wood

Foot bridge

River Wear

Finchale Priory

Finchale Abbey Caravan Park

Finchale Banks

3

2

infested" spot for over 50 years; he would only eat food when it was rotten and his bread was made half from flour and half from ashes. If things were not difficult enough he was almost killed by a band of fierce raiding Scots in 1138, and in 1149 his home was almost washed away by a flood. In spite of this asceticism he died on 21st May 1170 at the age of 105, and was buried in his oratory. After his death Finchale was occupied by two monks from Durham, one of whom, Reginald, was the biographer.

In 1241 the Archbishop of York ordered the building of a church at Finchale and this became a "holiday home" for the monks of Durham who came on a rota system, four at a time, to join the five resident monks.

Finchale Priory.

Unfortunately their behaviour seems to have been somewhat less than holy because they were severely reprimanded for keeping a pack of hounds for sport, wearing linen shirts instead of their monks' gowns, and other naughty habits...

However, in the general upheaval that came with the Dissolution of the Monasteries, St Godric's body vanished and today the site of his empty tomb is marked by a simple stone cross set into the floor of the nave.

The undercroft – Finchale Priory.

(1) After leaving the Priory ruins turn right and cross the wooden footbridge over the River Wear. A shallow ford at this point would have allowed the monks to cross the river to acess the woodland. Turn right at the end of the bridge and follow the broad riverside path —

River Wear near Finchale

Finchale woodland walk.

small areas of sand allow access to the river along this stretch.

There are several excellent specimens of the attractive but highly poisonous yew trees among the mature trees of this woodland walk. These were once considered sacred trees and it was thought they offered protection from malevolent spirits. During the Middle Ages it was used as a cardiac stimulant, and an abortifacient. It was also

A sinister yew tree.

put to use as a poison, used for assassination, suicide, as an arrow poison, and to poison fish and mammals. Nowadays its leaves are processed to extract Taxol, an anti-cancer drug which stops cell mutation. The berries have both a diuretic and laxative effect.

 Eventually the path forks, just in front of a large tree stump

— take the path to the left to climb the rustic steps and a gentle hill to a wooden bench.

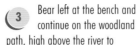 Bear left at the bench and continue on the woodland path, high above the river to

eventually exit onto a lay-by beside a minor road. Turn left between the walls and descend the steep steps to return to the riverside and cross the wooden bridge over the Wear back to the starting point.

Finchale Abbey footbridge.

2 **Durham River Banks Walk**

GR 273422

A walk around the wooded banks of the River Wear

This pleasant walk of just over two-and-a-half miles is rich in interest and should take about 45 minutes, not allowing for stops and diversions, to complete.

It starts from the north door of Durham Cathedral — note the

Level: 🥾
Length: Just over 2½ miles.
Duration: Approx 45 minutes.
Park and Start: Numerous car parks in Durham City. Cathedral parking restricted. NZ273421.
Refreshments: The Undercroft Restaurant in the Cathedral or the Alms Houses Restaurant on the Palace Green or at one of the numerous pubs, cafes or restaurants in Durham.

striking knocker — grasping this would provide any felon with the right to 37 days' sanctuary from their persecutors, the only crime that did not qualify for the "peculiar sanctuary" offered by Durham Cathedral was, of course, sacrilege.

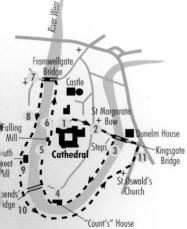

Durham Cathedral.

1 From the Cathedral door take the right hand of the two paths, and turn right at its end. Follow the footpath along the front of the Cathedral and straight ahead down the very narrow cobbled street.

This is Dun Cow Lane and it takes its name from the relief carving high on the nearby Cathedral wall which commemorates the legend of how a dairy maid searching for her dun cow helped a group of monks find the final resting place for the body of St Cuthbert.

2 Exit from Dun Cow lane and cross the road diagonally – taking great care – to go down the cobbled Bow Lane to the right of the small church of St Mary-le-Bow –

The misnamed Little Count's House.

now the Durham Heritage Centre. Turn right by the last house on the right and descend the steep flight of steps to the riverside.

3 An easy stroll along the riverside past the college boat houses, just where the path broadens out and bifurcates, is a small building on the right, which is sometimes wrongly called the Little Count's House. It's correct name is in fact Shipperdson's Cottage and it was built as a summerhouse for one of the

houses high up on the nearby steep wooded hillside. Count Josef Boruwalski did have a house in this area of the river banks but it was demolished sometime around 1850, after his death. He was a quite remarkable man – he was of Polish descent and a dwarf only 3'3" tall. He was well respected in Durham society as an intellectual and a talented musician who enjoyed the company of royalty and nobility. He died at the great age of 97 and is buried near the north door of Durham Cathedral.

4 Take the left hand fork in the path and continue straight ahead to pass under Prebends' Bridge. On the left of the path is a striking sculpture by Colin Wilbourne – "Cathedra" an interpretation and

Prebends' Bridge.

representation of the Bishop's Throne from which a cathedral takes its name.

Follow the path along by two college boathouses – the Pink House on the other side of the river was South Street Mill, where the locals brought their corn to be ground in the mill, operated by the Priory of Durham – or rather by a miller working for the Monks – it is probably safe to assume they just took the profit.

 5 Climbing the small incline with the rustic steps leads to the Fulling Mill which is now the Museum of Archaeology and also belonged to the Priory of Durham. It dates from the start of the 15th century and was a part of the newly established weaving trade which was then growing in the city.

6 Once past the Fulling Mill it is a pleasant riverside walk

South Street Mill.

Framwellgate bridge.

along a beautiful avenue of mature trees to climb the steps to Silver Street and turn left to cross Framwellgate Bridge.

This once carried one of the main roads into the city. The original was built in 1126 by Bishop Flambard but it was badly damaged by floods in the 1400s and had to be repaired and strengthened by Bishop Langley. The gatehouse which stood at the eastern end was removed in 1760 to ease the flow of traffic.

7 Descend the steps, by the public house, to the riverside and go straight ahead.

8 The views of the Castle and Cathedral opened out from this side of the river are excellent. Continue on to South Street Mill and the view from the paved area in front of the mill is the classic view, famous the world over, of Durham Cathedral high on the wooded river above the Fulling Mill with the River Wear flowing over the weir in the foreground.

9 The path leads through a walled passage to eventually climb towards Prebends' Bridge.

Interestingly, part of one of the old eastern spires from the Chapel of the Nine Altars of Durham Cathedral has been reconstructed here as a work called, "the Camera Obscura".

Cross the road. Follow the wide footpath staying on the same side of the river to eventually climb a set of stone steps into St Oswald's churchyard. The church dates from the 12th century

Kingsgate Bridge.

Street lamp and the Rose window, Durham Cathedral.

but was rebuilt in 1834 to a design by the noted architect Ignatius Bonomi.

10 Exit the churchyard and continue down Church Street to turn immediately left before the large concrete building of Dunelm House to cross Kingsgate Bridge back into Bow Lane.

Kingsgate Bridge was designed by the award winning architects Ove Arup and opened in 1963. It was constructed in two halves parallel to the river bank and when completed they were cleverly turned and locked into place.

11 From Bow Lane retrace the outward journey to arrive back at the north door of Durham Cathedral.

3 **Houghall Circular Walk**

GR 288411

Mature woodland, old railway tracks and riverside

Level: 🥾
Length: 3 miles.
Duration: Approx 1½ hours
Park and Start: Car park beside Shincliffe Bridge. NZ285411.
Refreshments: The nearby Rose Tree Inn, The Pumphouse Restaurant, or the Country Coffee Shop or The Seven Stars pub in Shincliffe Village.

This three mile walk takes a circular route around the old industrial village of Houghall, of which now there are scant remains. It was situated approximately 1.5 miles (2.4 km) to the south of Durham City centre and is the location of part of East Durham Colleges', Houghall Campus. Coal was mined from the Hutton seam in Houghall from 1840 and the colliery village built during the 1860s. Mining declined from the 1880s and the village was demolished in the 1950s when the area was land-scaped and turned over to picturesque woodland, although the foundations of some mining houses can still be seen in the woodland. It is a pleasant stroll along a riverside path and through some beautiful mature woodland. Mid May is probably the best time to do this walk when the woodland floor is covered with masses and masses of bluebells.

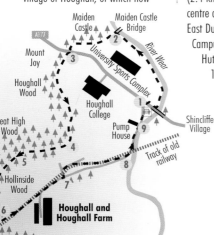

Maiden Castle
Maiden Castle Bridge
A177
River Wear
Mount Joy
University Sports Complex
Houghall Wood
Houghall College
Great High Wood
Pump House
Shincliffe Village
Track of old railway
Hollinside Wood
Houghall and Houghall Farm

River Wear at Shincliffe.

Great High Wood.

① Park in the small car park on the side road to the northwest of Shincliffe Bridge. Cross the A177 with great care and take the public footpath opposite that leads alongside the River Wear. Follow this footpath to eventually pass the unusual Maiden Castle footbridge to the kissing gate into the woodland.

Great High Wood.

② Once through the gate turn left and continue on the wide woodland path that skirts Maiden Castle, an Iron Age promontory fort, listed as a Scheduled Ancient Monument. The name Maiden Castle is not unique to this particular site and is found in several places in Britain; some historians take it to mean a "fortification that looks impregnable" or, possibly, one that has never been taken in battle.

3 Eventually this footpath arrives back at the A177 — again cross with great care and continue into the woodland on the other side of the road following the public footpath sign past the five bar gate.

4 Eventually we come to a picket fence that runs along the left hand side of the path — this marks the grounds of the Old Isolation Hospital. The building had various uses — was originally the village school and was only used as a hospital in the 1930s, but by 1946 it was used as accommodation for students attending the agricultural college until 1956 when it was demolished. The field still bears the name of "Hospital Field".

University sports field.

5 Continue straight ahead to where the path bifurcates at the top of a small rise near a welcome bench. Take the left fork downhill to continue through the wood. This wood was given to Durham University as

Houghall Wood.

Bluebells in the wood.

part of his endowment by William van Mildert, Bishop of Durham, in 1836.

The magnificent oaks and beeches of this ancient woodland provide a home for a wide variety of birds and woodland creatures including deer, foxes, squirrels and woodpeckers, which is quite remarkable in that it is only a mile from the centre of Durham City.

6 At the end of the woodland path climb the six wooden steps and turn left onto the Old Waggonway. Westwards the railway linked Houghall Colliery to Croxdale Colliery, where there was a brick and tile works, and to the east it linked with Shincliffe. The large depression part of the way along the embankment

was caused when the tunnel for the footpath to Durham collapsed — it now provides an interesting obstacle but mind your head when ducking under the tree that has fallen into the gap!

7 Leave the waggonway by crossing a wide stile onto a tarmac road. Go straight ahead to the end of the high hawthorn hedge on your left and turn left onto another road and almost immediately fork right. After about 150 metres turn right into the wood through a narrow

Bluebells in the wood

gap in the fence bearing a sign "Houghall Discovery Trail". Bear left on the lower path along the board-walk and climb the rustic staircase back onto the railway waggonway. Continue along the embankment to eventually exit from the Discovery Trail and the old railway, through an offset fence onto the tarmac road once again.

8 A short diversion to the right, along the road, in the first field on the left, is the famous Shincliffe Canyon. Extensive flooding in July 2009 caused the River Wear to break its banks and millions of gallons of water ripped through the soil in a cornfield owned by Houghall Agricultural College. Within seven hours the water had

The old pit heap – seen from Houghall.

drained away leaving an empty canyon 100 feet wide , 600 feet long and 15 feet deep – a testament to the awesome power of nature.

9 Return to the car park along the tarmac road passing the Old Pumphouse, a restaurant housed in the Victorian pumphouse, which once supplied Durham's water.

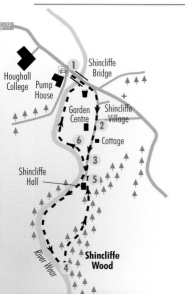

4 **Shincliffe Woods Walk**

GR 288411

*A beautiful stroll from the quiet village of
Shincliffe alongside the River Wear*

This is a pleasant 3½ mile walk past the 18th century Shincliffe Hall, alongside the River Wear and through the mature deciduous trees of Shincliffe Wood, easily completed in 1½ hours at a leisurely pace.

1 The walk starts from the small car park on the north-western side of Shincliffe Bridge. Cross the bridge and pass (or not!) the Rose Tree public house on the right and walk along the pavement into Shincliffe Village.

Shincliffe Woods in autumn.

Level:
Length: 3½ miles.
Duration: Approx 1½ hours.
Park and Start: Car Park on the north western side of Shincliffe Bridge. NZ285411
Refreshments: The nearby Rose Tree Inn, The Pumphouse Restaurant, or the Country Coffee Shop or The Seven Stars pub in Shincliffe Village.

23

The River Wear near Shincliffe Woods.

the river which can be seen down to the right.

Shincliffe Hall appears directly ahead and take the block-paved footpath alongside the new wrought-iron fence to the right of the building.

Cornfield.

2 Once in the village look out for the children's playground on the right just where the road bears left towards the middle of the village. Take the lane straight ahead sign-posted "Poplar Tree Garden Centre".

3 Follow the narrow road passing a small cottage on the left to where there is a small woodland; at the corner of a wood go through the gate onto a path that leads through the trees high above

The homeward track.

Go through the next gate and continue on the path which curves slightly downhill to join the river; continue on the path keeping the hedgerow on the left and the river to the right.

4 Once into the edge of Shincliffe Wood turn left and follow the well-defined path to Shincliffe Hall.

5 At the gate turn right onto the road to climb gently though the woodland before descending to the edge of the wood. Just where the road bends to the right away from the trees go through a small gap in the fence to follow the field edge with the River Wear on the left.

6 Eventually this path leads to a disused railway embankment, covered in trees. Go past the bridge abutment remains but stay on the footpath and onto the floodbank which leads back to the Rose Tree car park beside Shincliffe Bridge. Turn left and cross the bridge back to the car park. Simple!

The railway bridge remains.

Shincliffe Hall

The present buildings called Shincliffe Hall, date from the 1820s when extensions added to an earlier 18th century building.

William Rudd, steward and recorder of Durham in 1764 until and 1767 was the first known occupant of the original house. Towards the end of the 18th century the house became the property of John Thomas Hendry Hopper, of Witton Castle — his family is reputed to have lived in the village of Shincliffe for about 300 years. In 1796 Hopper sold the house to William Hutton of Carleton Hall, Cumberland.

Lt. John Prince and Isabella Cradock married in 1821 and occupied a small house on the site but,using money from Isabella's dowry, Prince extended part of this existing Manor House to create what he called Shincliffe Hall, the first use of the name.

The other, older house on the site was occupied the Hutton family who subsequently sold it in 1840 to John Henderson of the Henderson Carpet Company in Durham. He was only there for a short time, and sold the house in 1842 to Thomas Crawford who in turn sold it to the Prince family, creating a single estate in 1852. John Prince became a Captain in the Royal Navy by 1821and fought at the Battle of Trafalgar. He retired with honours in 1855.

After Captain Prince's death in 1869

the Hall was bought by the Dean and Chapter of Durham Cathedral for about £9,500 because they already held the mineral rights to the land.

The Dean and Chapter Cerk lived at the Hall. He was a solicitor called Richardson Peele who was also a secretary to three Bishops of Durham and a councillor, and he eventually became Mayor of Durham in 1889. The Hall had several owners up to World War II when it housed Land Army girls. After the war it was bought by Durham University for use student accommodation, at first by Hatfield College, and then the Graduate Society (now Ustinov College) up until October 2004. The hall is now in private ownership.

Shincliffe Hall.

Shincliffe Village

Shincliffe village stands beside the River Wear just to the south of Durham – it takes its name from the Old English word 'Scinna Cliffe', meaning the hill of the ghost or demon – it is not known exactly how this area came to be associated with demons and ghosts but the Anglo-Saxons certainly have a reputation of having been a superstitious race. Shincliffe was first recorded in AD 1085 as 'Scinneclif', when Bishop Carileph gave the area to the Prior and Convent of Durham. There is, however, evidence of occupation in the area from long before the medieval period. The earliest object to be found is a simple flint knife discovered near Manor Farm and probably dating from the Bronze Age.

There is some evidence for a Roman presence in the vicinity of Shincliffe. A Roman road, linking the Tees and the Tyne is thought to have passed near to a Roman villa which was sited at the nearby a Old Durham.

Shincliffe seems to have always been important with respect to river crossings and there have been several bridges at this site since the end of the 12th century. Bridge building was mentioned in 1368, but by 1385 it was said to be in a ruined state. Bishop Skirlaw built a new bridge in 1405 but this was destroyed and rebuilt in the mid 1500s. This new bridge was washed away in the great floods of 1773 and replaced by another which survived until 1824, when the present bridge was built.

Shincliffe Bridge.

5 **Observatory Hill Walk**

GR 273422

From Durham Cathedral to Observatory Hill and back

This is a short but enjoyable walk that starts and ends at Durham Cathedral. It is about three miles and should take about two hours to complete, allowing for several fairly stiff climbs.

Level: ♥ ♥

Length: 3 miles.

Duration: Approx 2 hours.

Park and Start: North door of Durham cathedral: NZ273421. Numerous car parks in Durham City. Cathedral parking is restricted

Refreshments: Undercroft Restaurant in the Cathedral or the Alms Houses Restaurant on the Palace Green, or at one of the numerous pubs, cafés or restaurants in Durham.

① Start from the north door of Durham Cathedral and follow the footpath to the University Music School, about 25 metres. Turn left down the "vennell", known as Windy Gap — it was here in the Divinity House (now the University Music School) that John Meade Falkner (1858–1932) the English novelist and poet, perhaps best known for his 1898 novel, *Moonfleet*, lived when he served as Honorary Librarian to the Dean and Chapter Library of Durham Cathedral. There is a commemorative plaque here, while his monument is in the south cloister of the cathedral.

Durham Cathedral from St Margaret's churchyard.

Turn right at the end of Windy Gap and walk down the fenced path, with Durham Castle high on your right, towards the riverside. At the end of this path climb the short flight of old stone steps between the buildings to come onto on Framwellgate Bridge. Turn left and cross the bridge.

The original was built by Ralph Flambard, Bishop of Durham, in the early 12th century as the first permanent River crossing – it was defended by a tower and gateway which were demolished in the mid 18th century.

The present bridge dates from the early 15th century and the episcopate of Bishop Langley.

St Margaret's Church.

South Street.

2 At the western end of the bridge follow the left fork of the road to climb Crossgate, past "the Fighting Cocks" one of Durham's oldest inns, and St Margaret's Church. Climb the second set of steps to arrive at the western entrance to the churchyard from upper Crossgate.

3 Follow the footpath through the churchyard to arrive at the end of a wall lined with old headstones. Take the unmade path to climb to the top of the old graveyard from where there is a magnificent view of Durham Cathedral and Castle.

Continue straight ahead on the footpath to exit the churchyard through a small doorway in a wall to arrive on South Street, one of the oldest streets

Durham Cathedral from Observatory Hill.

in Durham, indeed it was once the main road south out of the city, hence its name.

Turn right and climb the cobbled street enjoying the views of the cathedral across the River valley to the left.

Continue to the top of South Street and into Pimlico, which was once the artists' quarter of the city, and thence follow a walled lane to a public footpath" sign on the right. Go up this short lane and ascend the steps to be faced with Durham School, across the road.

Durham School was founded almost six hundred years ago as an independent day and boarding school for girls and boys and has nearly 650

boys and girls from age 3 to 18. Unlike most schools, however, Durham School operates a house system; all students are members of a house. Alumni, referred to as Old Dunelmians, are found across the

Durham School.

spectrum of public life, the armed services, the arts, the church and in sport.

(4) Take geat care in crossing the road and continue on the footpath around the outside of the school along Quarry Heads Lane to a public footpath sign and a Durham Archery Club sign which directs along a roughly made road to arrive at another public footpath sign. Turn left here and climb the leafy lane. At the summit of the climb go straight on at the junction, keeping the sports fields to the left.

(5) Where the path bifurcates continue to bear left to eventually come out at the Observatory.

The Observatory.

This a weather observatory owned and operated by the University of Durham. It is a Grade II listed building and was founded in 1839, initially as an astronomical and meteorological observatory, until 1937 when its purpose became purely meteorological recording. After the Radcliffe Observatory in Oxford, Durham has the longest unbroken meteorological record of any University in the UK, with records dating back to the 1840s. Nowadays the observatory contributes to the Met Office's forecasts by providing automated records.

(6) Follow the narrow lane that runs alongside the observatory to cross a stile into a field offering excellent views of Durham School and the southern aspect of Durham Cathedral.

Go down the field toward the facing end of an old hawthorn hedge, follow this old hedge for about a 100 metres, keeping it on the left and exit this field by crossing two consecutive stiles in the fence.

(7) Follow the hedge on the left, skirting a small attractive hillock with four mature trees to arrive at a metal gate with a stile to the left. Climb this stile and cross a small utility field to go through a gateway by a public footpath sign back onto Quarry Heads Lane.

Turn right and in about 25 metres cross the road, with great care, to some white gates beside a gatehouse cottage. Go through the gates and descend the old lane, bearing right past the small Bankman's Cottage and down the slope to cross Prebends' Bridge.

Prebends' Bridge was designed by architect George Nicholson in 1777 to

The Banksman's Cottage.

replace an earlier version dating from 1696 which was washed away in the Great Flood of 1771. It affords what is considered by many to be one of the finest views of the towers of Durham Cathedral.

On the northern parapet at the western end of the bridge is an inscription written by Sir Walter Scott about the cathedral: "Grey towers of Durham, Yet well I love thy mixed and massive piles, Half church of God half castle against the Scot, And long to roam these venerable aisles, With records stored of deeds long since forgot". It is thought by some historians that he dashed these poetic words off on a serviette while waiting for his pudding when he was attending at a dinner in Durham Castle as a guest of Bishop Barrington.

The Ramp.

8 On crossing the bridge turn left and take the right fork in the path to climb towards The Ramp. At the top of the path bear right through the open gate to climb The Ramp, which leads into the dark entry, an eerie entrance into the college grounds behind the cathedral and the end of the walk.

What better way to finish such a pleasant walk than a visit to Durham Cathedral?

6 Shincliffe Bridge Circular Walk GR 275423

A delightful four mile riverside stroll

This is an easy four mile walk from Durham City to and from the nearby village of Shincliffe along opposite sides of the River Wear.

① The walk starts at the Riverside below Elvet Bridge which was built in the 12th century during the episcopy of Bishop Pudsey and linked the suburb of Elvet to Saddler Street and the Market Place. From Elvet Bridge follow the riverside footpath westwards to Baths Bridge.

Level: ♥ ♥
Length: 4 miles.
Duration: Approx 2½ hours
Park and Start: Numerous car parks in Durham City. NZ275426.
Refreshments: At any of the numerous pubs, cafés or restaurants in Durham.

Durham Cathedral from Pelaw Wood.

35

2 This is the third Baths Bridge on this site – the first was built of wood in 1855 and replaced by a girder bridge in 1898 which in turn was replaced by the present concrete arch, a copy of the original, in 1962. Carry straight on along the towpath with the College of St Hild and St Bede on your left; These were once the teachers' training colleges of St Hild and St Bede, but are now part of Durham University. Continue to arrive at Pelaw Wood.

3 Cross the small bridge into Pelaw Wood. This wood was presented to the City of Durham by Lord Londonderry in the 1930s. Unfortunately the pathways and bank sides were eroding into the river and so a strong retaining wall was built to solve the problem.

Baths Bridge.

4 Carry on through the wood, following the curve of the river to emerge at a point known as "Drummer Boy's Hole". The Durham City Rowing Club buildings can be seen on the opposite bank.

Drummer Boy's Hole

In the late 1700s the ford across the River at the eastern end of Pelaw Wood was quite dangerous and great care had to be taken when crossing. A story from this time recounts how, on a winter's evening during a particularly murky dusk, a young Drummer Boy with the Durham Militia missed his footing during crossing and stumbled into a hole in the riverbed and drowned in the icy water, in spite of frantic attempts by his fellows to rescue him. It is said that, at dusk on a winter's evening, when the conditions are right, the sound of drumbeats can be heard as the ghost of the unfortunate boy tries to pick his way over the treacherous ford.

5 From this point, where three paths diverge, take the right hand side one to the Kingfisher Bridge. This, bridge crosses Old Durham Beck and was opened on the 18 December 2007 at a cost of £125,000.

6 From the bridge carry on along the path to pass through the remains of the Elvet Railway Bridge which carried the Durham to Sunderland line across the Wear at this point.

Paws on the Kingfisher Bridge.

Elvet Railway

In 1893 the North Eastern Railway opened a station in Elvet in Durham city. This was served by a new line branching off the old Shincliffe line at Sherburn House. However the passenger service to Elvet was not a great success and had a short life of less than 40 years as it was withdrawn on 1 January 1931. The station continued to be used for one day a year (except during the war years) until 18 July 1953. The one day was the famous Durham Miners' Gala and on this day special trains were run from most of the surrounding pit villages, bringing miners, their families, bands and banners to the city. One of the last uses of Elvet Station was by a circus that came by train in 1953.

Maiden Castle Bridge.

Shincliffe Bridge.

7. The path now curves gently to the left as it passes the impressive mound of Maiden Castle

across the river and arrives at Maiden Castle Footbridge. This bridge was designed by the award-winning

Maiden Castle from the railway bridge remains.

Maiden Castle river banks.

architects Ove Arup & Company in 1972 and links the University Sports Hall with the rugby and football pitches across the river. Cross the bridge, turn left and follow the riverside path to eventually come out on Shincliffe Bridge.

 8 Turn left and cross the river by this bridge and turn

immediately left, pass through a metal gate and follow the unmade road back to Maiden Castle Bridge.

The wide open spaces of the sports field provide a wonderful opportunity to throw a ball for your dog, and if you haven't a dog get one!

 9 Cross Maiden Castle Bridge again, turn right onto the

unmade path that winds along the base of Maiden Castle Fort. The fort is on top of the hill about a hundred feet above the surrounding countryside. Substantial remains are clearly visible at the western end of the summit — there is the trace of a circular wall surrounded by a large ditch almost 30 feet wide which would probably have been crossed by a drawbridge.

Cricket match — University sports field.

10 The path continues to the remains of the Elvet Railway Bridge on the south bank of the river. Bear left and almost immediately turn right onto an unmade track though a small larch wood, keeping the allotments to your right.

11 This brings you to a metalled road which should be crossed with great care.

After crossing the road, turn right along the unmade road and follow this past the Rowing Club buildings to a gate and go straight on.

This area is known as "The Racecourse" — it was first mentioned in 1773, although racing horses here actually dates back to 1665. Race

The Durham Cow sculpture.

meetings were held twice a year in April and July until 1887 when they clashed with the Durham Miners' Big Meeting. In 1888 the Race Committee surrendered their lease to the University and the course was closed, but by then a number of officials in

The Bandstand.

the city thought that the races "had degenerated into a very disreputable affair". A new racecourse was built at Shincliffe.

Walk along the river bank passing the bandstand — and "the Durham Cow", a public sculpture by Andrew Burton. A cow features in the legend of the discovery of Dunholm by Lindisfarne Monks searching for a final resting place for the body of St Cuthbert; we are led to believe however that this cow was a roan Durham shorthorn.

12 Follow the wide path past the University Sports grounds to Baths Bridge. Cross and turn left and this will bring you back to Elvet Bridge — your starting point for this refreshing four mile walk.

7 **Kepier Wood Walk**

GR 274428

An old hospital, a shooting range and a quarry

This pleasant walk is just under 5 miles in length and should take about 2½ hours to complete. It is a varied medium level walk following the valley of the River Wear to the east of Durham City. It starts from The Sands Car Park in Durham City.

1 Leave the car park on the track at the north-east corner to walk through a pleasant copse of trees to the area known as The Sands. This large open area on the edge of the city is supported by the Freemen of Durham who, and if they so wish, can enjoy the privilege of grazing their goats here!

2 Follow the footpath with the River Wear to the left to come out onto a roadside track just opposite the street

Level: ♥ ♥
Length: Just under 5 miles.
Duration: Approx 2½ hours.
Park and Start: The Sands Car Park. NZ275430.
Refreshments: At any of the numerous pubs, cafés or restaurants in Durham.

The River Wear in Kepier Wood.

Map labels:

Kepier Wood
Elfin Bridge
Frankland Farm
Frankland Wood
River Wear
Shooting Range
Kepier Quarries
Crook Hall
enny erry idge
The Sands
School
Kepier: remains of hospital
A690

6 5 7 4 8 9 2 3 1

marked "Ferens Close". Follow this roadside track, keeping a watchful eye for traffic to go through a gate with a nearby sign — "Kepier Farm Estates".

3 Follow this farm road to Kepier Hospital — an old leper hospital once run by the monks of Durham Cathedral. Cross the stile straight ahead and take the path which leads along by a long bend in the river. Pass through a narrow gateway beside the football pitches on the right and continue straight on to a double stile. Cross this stile and make left on a track which leads through a

An unusual double stile.

Kepier Hospital.

patch of hawthorn scrub. Soon the path forks — take the right hand fork to eventually climb some rustic steps to the edge of a large field sloping down to the river. Follow the path downhill toward the river and make for two concrete walls in the distance.

Kepier Wood.

The old shooting range.

The new Elfin Bridge.

These are the remains of a rifle range where the Durham Light Infantry used to practice just before and during World War II.

From the old rifle range, keeping the River to the left, make for the woodland straight ahead.

 4 Cross the stile into Kepier Wood and follow the winding woodland track to arrive, after a short climb to a concrete and green tubular steel bridge over a ravine.

5 Cross this bridge and continue on the well-defined woodland track. Look out for signs of quarrying to your right and also look out for old filled in level mouths, a reminder of the industry that was carried on in these woods.

Site of the old fish garth at Kepier.

Eventually the path leads to the Elfin Bridge – this is so named because it replaced the previous rickety bridge because of Elf 'n' safety.

6 Once safely over the bridge take the right fork where the path bifurcates and climb gently through the wood for about 100 yards and then, where the path joins another, turn sharp right and continue on a steeper path to climb out of the wood. Exit the wood and carry on along the field edge, with a small stream valley on your right. This path eventually arrives at a stile in the fence just below the embankment of the main A690 Durham to Sunderland road.

7 Cross the stile, turn right, and climb gently to reach the level of the road and continue along an easy and pleasant wooded path to arrive at a small car park with picnic area.

Exit the car park by the path at the far right hand corner and descend into the wood again. At the bottom of the slope is the green bridge but don't cross – turn sharp left to rejoin the inward path.

8 Follow this route back to the edge of Kepier Wood and

cross the stile once more but take the raised path, keeping the fence to the left, and rejoin the path through the scrub at the rustic steps.

(9) Arriving back at the double stile cross and go straight ahead on the road along the edge of the Northern Electric Kepier Training Area. The old building on the left at the end of the road is all that remains of the old Kepier Brickworks, and its adjacent and supposedly bottomless pond.

The road leads back to Kepier Hospital and from here retrace the route along The Sands back to the car park.

Milburngate Bridge and Durham Cathedral.

Kepier oaks in autumn.

8 **Frankland Walk**

GR:273429

A stroll along what is also known as "Brian's Walk"

This pleasant walk starts from the edge of the centre of Durham City and follows a figure of eight out to a series of attractive ponds and local nature reserve to return to the city.

① The walk begins at the Pennyferry Bridge which takes its name from the fact that a ferry once worked here, and the ferryman charged a penny for his services. The bridge was opened in April 2002 by the local MP, Gerry Steinberg. The ceremony was complete with a brass band, and old pennies were presented to the first twenty people to cross the bridge, in commemoration of the penny fare paid on the old ferry.

Level: 🥾 🥾
Length: 4.6 miles.
Duration: Just under two hours.
Park and Start: On Framwellgate Waterside on the eastern Durham City, starting from north side of the Pennyferry Bridge opposite the Radisson Hotel. There is a large car park on the south side of the bridge. NZ275430.
OS map: Explorer 308 or Pathfinder 572.
Refreshments: Many hotels, pubs, restaurants, and coffee shops in Durham City

Map labels: HM Prison, Brasside Ponds, Low Newton Junction Nature Reserve, Disused Railway, The Scroggs, London–Edinburgh Railway Line, **Frankland Farm**, Pennyferry Bridge, Durham Castle, Durham Cathedral

The Pennyferry Bridge.

From the bridge follow the riverside footpath a short way to a small roundabout and continue north-east along a tarmac road first passing Crook Hall with its splendid gardens and then Frankland Cottage.

Crook Hall is a fine example of three periods of English architecture — medieval, Jacobean and Georgian. The Medieval Hall dates from 1208, the Jacobean Mansion was built in 1671 and the Hopper family built the Georgian House in 1720. The main hall was restored about thirty years ago and it is said the circular turret was added to allow the ancient wooden stairs to remain in place — for the sole use by the ghost of the White Lady, who is said to haunt the room. She was the niece of the irascible Cuthbert BIllingham who famously cut off Durham's water supply in 1631.

(2) Turn left at the signpost indicating "Newton Hall 1¼ miles", pass the Barkers Haugh Treatment Works on the left, and come out onto an unfenced road which crosses open farmland, and eventually leads to another footpath sign.

The path follows the Weardale Way.

Frankland Farm.

(3) Climb this tarmac road, keeping the hedgerow on the right, which eventually leads to a white farm house. About forty yards before the house the road bears to the right to a gate. From here there is an excellent view, back towards the city and Durham Cathedral. Cross the stile to the right of the gate and follow the road keeping the old farm buildings on the left.

(4) This is now Frankland Lane — follow this track between the farm buildings and a white bungalow

The view from Frankland Farm.

towards Newton Hall. At the junction go straight ahead to follow the unmade wooded footpath as it climbs past the ancient Oak wood – The Scrogs – and on along a pleasant wooded lane to arrive at a junction with another track on the right just before the Dovecote Farm Boarding Kennels and Cattery.

5 Follow this rutted, winding track past an old cattle crush

Looking to Durham Cathedral from Frankland Lane.

and between two old railway bridge supports to a facing field gate. At the field gate turn left onto a narrow, winding track that leads anti-clock-wise around the edge of Brasside Ponds. Care must be taken on this uneven track which can be slippy, during, or just after, wet weather.

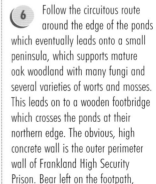

6 Follow the circuitous route around the edge of the ponds which eventually leads onto a small peninsula, which supports mature oak woodland with many fungi and several varieties of worts and mosses. This leads on to a wooden footbridge which crosses the ponds at their northern edge. The obvious, high concrete wall is the outer perimeter wall of Frankland High Security Prison. Bear left on the footpath, crossing two stiles, eventually coming out through the remains of a gate onto a narrow road and turn left towards Frankland Junction.

7 There are still traces of the old railway crossing at Frankland Junction where Frankland Lane once crossed the old Durham to Sunderland Railway line. At this point turn right at an acute angle to follow the old trackbed of the disused railway.

8 Follow this old railway track, passing through Low Newton Junction Local Nature Reserve, to come out at the Durham to Newton Hall footpath. Turn left and walk downhill back to the farms.

9 From the farms keep left on the road downhill, which will eventually lead back past the treatment works to the Pennyferry Bridge.

Brasside Ponds
The two ponds at Brasside form one of the largest open water habitats in lowland County Durham.

Brasside ponds.

This part of the valley of the River Wear has deep, laminate clays which were excavated on a large scale early in the 20th century. Several clay ovens operated at Brasside between 1900 and 1920, but many of their clay pits were filled in with Durham City's domestic waste, although a remaining couple became flooded to form the existing ponds.

Mute swan.

Coot and chick (or cooting).

There are geese, coots, grebes and both diving and dabbling ducks all present on the ponds but the largest numbers are, naturally, seen in winter. Also to be seen are many other birds such as warblers, goldcrests, gulls, waders and herons.

The ponds are equally important for aquatic insects, with large numbers of damselflies, dragonflies, alderflies, caddisflies and mayflies.

Low Newton Junction Local Nature Reserve

Low Newton Junction Local Nature Reserve is a protected grassland habitat and important local wildlife site. This delicate habitat is renowned for its precarious colony of Great Crested Newts and is a haven for solitary bees and wasps, especially important as pollinators, and which nest in holes rather than communal hives. The Dingy Skipper can also be found here – this small, rare brown butterfly can be seen mainly in Spring, basking in the sunshine on bare patches of ground with its wings spread wide. In dull weather, and at night, it perches on the tops of dead flowerheads in a moth-like fashion with wings curved in a position that is not seen in any other British butterfly.

9 **Bearpark Walk**

GR 267428

An impressive viaduct and atmospheric medieval ruins

This six mile walk leaves Durham City from Waddington Street, in the shade of the impressive Victorian Viaduct.

(1) At the end of Waddington Street go through the entrance archway of the King's Lodge Hotel

and follow the public footpath into Flass Vale Local Nature Reserve. Eventually descend a flight of steps and continue straight ahead to exit the reserve into Flassburn Road. From the end of this road turn left at the T-junction into Fieldhouse Lane. In about a hundred yards turn left into Springfield Park. On the first bend of the road there is a footpath which leads to the A167 straight opposite Club Lane bridleway. Cross the road with great care and follow the bridleway along a hedged lane and field

Level: 🐾 🐾
Length: 6 miles.
Duration: 3 hours.
Park and Start: Start opposite United Reform Church in Waddington Street. NZ 267427. Numerous car parks in Durham City.
Refreshments: Any of the numerous pubs, cafés or restaurants in Durham.

Flass Vale.

Club Lane.

edges to a gate onto a farm track. Turn right and follow this road to eventually cross the River Browney just below the ruins of Beaurepaire. It is most certainly worth making a small detour to see the ruins more closely.

(2) The medieval estate of Beaurepaire – translated as beautiful retreat – was created by the Prior of Durham Cathedral when the Bishop gave permission to enclose 1300 acres of adjacent land in the mid 1200's. At the Dissolution of the

The extensive remains of Beaurepaire

Durham Priory in 1539 the estate passed to the Dean and Chapter. The centre of the estate was the Prior's residence which was built in 1258 and for many years it was used as a country retreat by both the Prior of Durham and his monks. Many important guests

Beaurepaire is a fine example of an old manor house

were received here including Edward I, on his way to "hammer the Scots", Edward II, after he was hammered by the Scots, and Edward III, who was a great friend and contemporary of Bishop Thomas Hatfield. Sixteen thousand Scots under King David camped here before their defeat at the Battle of Neville's Cross on 17 October 1346.

The north wing probably contained the main hall and kitchen while the south wing housed the Prior's private apartments. The remaining ruins visible today were the large dormitory, Beaurepaire is regarded as one of the most extensive manor house sites in the North of England.

These lands once belonged to the Prior of Durham Cathedral

From the ruins descend to cross the bridge over the River Browney, and continue up the track to meet the Lanchester Valley railway path.

(3) On reaching the railway path turn left, enjoy the view of Beaurepaire across the valley to the left, and follow this path to cross a road before reaching Aldin Grange Farm. Continue past Aldin Grange on the railway path to where it crosses

a farm road with an ornate black signpost. Turn left and go through the facing gate into the yard of Baxter Wood Farm — continue through the farm to walk downhill to a small bridge across the River Browney. Continue straight ahead up a gentle climb to arrive at Tollhouse Road. Cross the road with great care and turn right to follow the footpath up to the traffic lights. Turn left here and continue to the footbridge. Cross the

Battle of Neville's Cross sculp
in the grounds of
Johnston Sch

Baxter Wood Farm.

Old horse trough, Baxter Wood Farm.

footbridge to continue past the Johnston School. At the end of the school fence turn right at the public footpath sign and follow the enclosed path down to Flass Vale.

(4) It was on the site where the Johnston School now stands that the Battle of Neville's Cross was fought on 17th October 1346. Five thousand English soldiers, under the command of Ralph Neville, Henry Percy and the Archbishop of York, defeated 16,000 Scots led by King David II and William Douglas. The battle was brief but bloody. The Scots' standard bearer, Alexander Ramsey was killed and King David was wounded and captured by John Copeland – the king's reflection in the water under Aldin Grange Bridge, where he was hiding, is said to have given him away. King David was taken to a Northumbrian castle to recover from his wounds and thence to the Tower of London – he was eventually ransomed for almost £70,000,

Durham Cathedral seen from Flass Vale.

today's equivalent of £15 million pounds — coincidentally the same amount as Newcastle United paid for Alan Shearer after Euro '96.

A sculpture was erected in the school grounds in 1996 as part of the 650th anniversary commemoration events. It was created by sculptor Graeme Hopper with staff and students and provides a fitting memorial for this significant battle.

(5) On reaching a junction in the path in the bottom of Flass Vale, turn sharp right, at an acute angle to follow a winding woodland path through the Vale. Eventually the path becomes a track and then a road which leads back to the start of the walk.

Flass Vale Local nature reserve was granted its status in March 2008. Grazing animals were kept in the vale until as recently as the 1960s but

Flass Vale.

since then this area of natural woodland has expanded — the formal gardens have overgrown and there are only traces of a once productive orchard. The 1860 Ordnance Survey map shows pasture, hedges, woodland and bog as making up the vale, and interestingly the upper part was flooded in winter to form a pond for ice skating and curling. This was the route that monks would take on their way to Beaurepaire — through this wonderful little hidden area, rich in plants and wildlife, bluebells, wood anemone, wood sorrel, foxglove, herb bennet, herb robert, wild raspberries, dog rose and yellow flag iris. And many species of birds have been recorded along with foxes, rabbits, badgers, and even deer.

10 **Pittington and Renny's Lane Walk** GR 325448

A walk around country lanes and disused railway tracks

This varied six and a half mile walk starts from the attractive little village of Low Pittington. The village grew from agriculture and, as its name would suggest, mining.

However, one of the most attractive things about this walk is the profusion and wide variety of wildflowers that can be seen in spring and summer, the pathways along the old railway lines are literally an explosion of colour throughout these seasons.

(1) Take Lady's Piece Lane, signposted "Hallgarth", from the crossroads near the Blacksmith's Arms. About fifty yards along this minor road is a public footpath sign pointing to the right. Cross the stile to join a long straight

Level: 🌸🌸
Length: 6½ miles.
Duration: 4 hours.
Park and Start: Parking in the village. Take care not to cause obstruction. NZ325448.
Refreshments: The Blacksmith's Arms or The Hallgarth Manor Hotel, just a short drive from the start — while visiting this hotel its well worth having a look at the nearby St Laurence Church.

path that leads to a metal gate with a wooden kissing gate to its

Rosebay willow herb.

Poppies bring a bright splash of colour to the walk.

right. Go through this gate and continue on through the next field between two open lines of large bushes to another stile, slightly to the right.

Climb over this style and cross a field for horses to yet another stile crossing onto what is obviously an old railway trackbed, that once carried the line from Elvet station in Durham to Murton, Easington and the coast.

(2) After about a mile a railway bridge, crossing the old track, comes into view; just before the bridge fork off left where the path divides, and climb gently to follow the track of a disused railway. Eventually this trackside path arrives at a small

The disused railway line.

The path leads alongside a disused railway line.

stile which crosses into a narrow field. Exit the field from the left-hand corner over a stile beside a heavily pad-locked gate and go along a short unmade lane to a minor road.

(3) Turn right and go past a Leisure Centre and playground to arrive at the main road.

(4) Turn right here and follow the footpath past Sherburn Woods to the far side of the railway bridge. Cross the road here and go onto the public footpath indicated by the sign next to the facing gate. Follow this wide, grassed field edge footpath as it curves gently down into a sunken lane, leading to a small metal bridge crossing Sherburn House Beck.

An excellent example of a sunken lane near Sherburn House.

5 From the bridge turn left and negotiate another stile, beside a large ash tree, onto a field edge path and climb steeply following the line of trees to exit this large field through an open gateway onto a footpath beside a road. Turn right and keep on this footpath to pass Sherburn Hospital, which once housed lepers but is now a retirement home with sheltered housing.

Descend into the little valley of the Sherburn House Beck, only to climb up the other side to eventually arrive at a T-junction.

6 Cross the road with great care at the T-junction and turn left and walk to a set of traffic lights. Turn right here and walk down this long

Harebells – Rennys lane.

A field edge path near Sherburn.

straight road to eventually arrive at the Gilesgate Moor Hotel and turn right onto Renny's Lane.

7 Carry straight on to eventually go through a motorway underpass to emerge onto a hedgerow-lined track. Follow this pleasant track gently downhill until it reaches a junction – take the centre path and make for the railway bridge ahead.

A friendly pony in Sherburn.

Part of the path follows an old railway trackbed.

8 About a hundred yards after the railway bridge rejoin the outward path to retrace the journey to Pittington, where hopefully, you'll be welcomed by the Blacksmith's 'Open' Arms to enjoy a well–deserved large ale on the rocks or a flagon of whiskey to quench the thirst!

Renny's Lane – a colourful display of flowers in summer.

Renny's Lane follows the route of an old road used by drovers, braggers, badgers, cadgers, salters and pie men on their way to the market in Durham from Pittington, Elemore, Hetton and the coast. Braggers were licenced by the 16th century Halifax Act to sell small amounts of wool they had collected fro outlying farms and villages. Badgers were the licenced peddlers who would carry their chaps or packs from homestead to homestead selling their wares. Spices, lace, ribbons and sewing materials, perfumes and simple medicines would all be laid out on the big kitchen tables in the farm houses where goods and gossip would be dispensed in equal measure...

Sherburn Hospital was built by Bishop Hugh Pudsey in the late 1100s to care for 65 monks and nuns suffering from leprosy. After the curse of this awful disease had eased a few patients suffering from other diseases were admitted for treatment, but by the 16th century the building had badly deteriorated and much rebuilding and renovation was carried out through Georgian and Victorian times. Today the building is a comfortable retirement and care home for gentlefolk.

Gatehouse – Sherburn Hospital.